Selling Goodwill Items On Ebay

How to Buy Low Form Goodwill And Sell High On eBay for Hugh Profit Margins

Sally Parker

Table of Content

Introduction

I want to thank you and congratulate you for purchasing this book. Selling Goodwill Items On eBay is actually easy to do, so long as you have a source you can continue to rely on.

This book contains proven steps and strategies on how to find low priced Goodwill items and sell them on eBay for a huge margins profit.

If you are looking for a way to make extra income or if you are looking for a real home based business then Goodwill and eBay are the way to go and this book will show you how you can do both.

Thanks again for buying this book, I hope you enjoy it!

How I got started

If you are looking for a way to make extra money or if you are looking for a real home based business, then Goodwill outlets and eBay are the way to go and this book will help you get started.

First a little about me. I have always been looking for a way to own my own home based business and work for myself, which would allow me to have more freedom. I've tried just about everything. I tried Amway and a few other pyramid programs in the late 80's, before the internet became a household item. Then again in the mid 90's when the internet was just starting to take off.

I purchased "how to eBook" after "how to eBook" in hopes of finding and starting my own online business, but I soon found out that none of those "how to eBooks" workout and where just a waste of time and money. So after a few years of that I gave up, I thought "Oh well, it's just not meant to be."

But in December of 2012 I ran across a YouTube video and in that video some guy was explaining how to sell house hold items on eBay, he was going to thrift stores and garage sales and finding items at a low price and then he would flip them onto eBay. He even mentioned going to Goodwill stores, not Goodwill outlets, but Goodwill stores, as you will see in this book, there is a big difference between Goodwill stores and Goodwill outlets. So I decided to give it a go. In the two years of selling items I have gathered a lot of experience, like which items will sell on eBay, which ones sell faster and so on. So I decided to put it all in a book and share what I have learned with you, so you too can learn the art of selling Goodwill items on eBay.

SIGNING UP WITH PAYPAL

The first thing you will want to do before you start any selling on eBay is to figure out how you would like to be paid. There are a several different ways to be paid, one is through PayPal and by far the most popular and in my opinion the best way. I will be covering PayPal, because this is what I use, but you can use other forms like PayPal credit, Skrill, Escrow and a few others, but you can go to eBay and check out all the payment methods eBay allows. Because this book is about showing you what I do, I will only be covering PayPal.

Signing up for PayPal is pretty simple, all you have to do is go to their website and decide if you want to register a personal account or a business account, both are free to set up. When registering with PayPal you will be asked for a user name and password, after you register you are going to want to add your personal bank account, this is so that PayPal will be able to verify who you are.

How PayPal verifies who you are, is pretty simple, what they do is deposit a few cents in to the bank account you have set up with PayPal, once they deposit the money, you simple go to your personal bank account, find the amount they added, then go back to PayPal and tell them how much they added, if the amount that you entered is correct then you are verified and ready to start selling on eBay and taking payments via PayPal.

Way back when eBay first hit the internet they would allow buyers to purchase items using money orders, but this is no longer allowed, which I think is great. The last thing you want as a seller is to be ripped off, and this is where PayPal comes in.

Just so you know eBay is owned by PayPal and they work hand in hand, eBay and PayPal have come a long way over the years, and as a seller on eBay you will have confidence knowing that they have set into place a lot of protection for sellers.

Over the past 2 years I have had a few cases where a buyer had bought an item from my eBay store and paid me via PayPal, the buyer, after receiving the item went over to PayPal and claimed they did not authorize the purchase, after receiving a email from PayPal, letting me know that a buyer had a claim open against me for the amount of the purchase price, I simple called up PayPal and gave them the tracking number, they looked up the purchase history which also shows the delivery history and it showed that the item was purchased on eBay via PayPal and that the item was indeed shipped to the address that the buyer has on file with eBay and PayPal, so PayPal released the hold on the amount for the purchase price.

When you make your very first sale on eBay, you will want to make sure that you have added the tracking number that you received from the shipping company you used, for example, I use USPS (United States Postal Service) but you can use which everyone you like, the point is, PayPal will not release any money to you until you have added a tracking number, but we will cover this in more detail in a later chapter, but for now this is enough info about PayPal to get you started..

ACCOUNT SIGN EBAY UP

Now that you have your PayPal account set up and verified the next thing you need to do is set up an account with eBay. Simple go to your browser and type in eBay and you will be taking to a screen where you can either log into your eBay account or sign up for one. When you register with eBay you will be asked for your name, email address and contact information. Once you have completed the information requested you will be sent a confirmation message via email, in that email eBay will have given you a ID which you can keep or change, to change your ID or any information you gave eBay, simply log into your account and go to My eBay, then click the Account tab and go to your personal information and change what you like. If you google "how to sign up for eBay" you will see eBay has all the information I just gave and more. Also don't forget to download eBay's free app for your Apple or Smartphone. You can sign up the old fashion way via your PC or Laptop, or you can do what all the cool kids are doing and just use their phone and eBay phone app. You will see how important having eBay's app is once you get started selling on eBay.

Ok now that you have your eBay account set up go into it and see if you need or want to make a changes to it. So sign in, go to my eBay, a drop down window will appear, click on summary, then account, now this is what I see when I am on my laptop or PC, in the account tab window, right below the My Account you will see the Change automatic payment method option. This is where you can decide how you want to pay your monthly eBay bill. Your bill will consist of listing fees and seller fees that you have accumulated in any giving month. I have this set up to be paid automatically via my PayPal account, simple because I use my PayPal account to purchase all my eBay selling materials, and PayPal is also how I get paid when someone makes a purchase from my eBay store. You don't have to do it this way, you can use your personal bank account, but for me it's simple and easy to track using my PayPal account. Now if you scroll down further in the same account window you will see the fees that eBay is charging you, right above that there is a link to make a one-time payment. I like to try and pay my eBay bill once a week, otherwise if you do a lot of selling on eBay, the monthly bill can sometimes be a shocker if you don't pay your fees regularly. Having a high bill will eBay is a good thing, it means you are selling a ton of items, and that is just the price of doing business and well worth it, because other than Amazon, I don't know of any other site that reaches more people around the world. If you were to try and reach the same amount of people that eBay does with your own website it would cost you a ton of money. I know a few people that did not like the fact that they had to pay eBay a fee for listing and selling, so they decided to go it on their own with either a blog or a website and failed miserable because they did not take into account that just because you have your own blog or website does not mean you are going to make a sale, you still have to market your website, you have to let people know that you have items online and that is where money and time come into play.. I for one do not have a ton of money to throw at marketing nor do I have the time to learn how to get free marketing, which also takes time and nor do I. I just want to find my products and list them, get paid, and ship the item. Why not let the experts at eBay worry about all that for you, and if you are worried about the fees eBay charges, you can always raise the price of your item a few dollars to help cover the cost, but remember eBay charges a percentage of the selling price, and that percentage varies based on if you have a eBay store, what type of eBay store or if you have no store at all, but we will cover this in more detail in the next chapter.

PICKING THE RIGHT EBAY ACCOUNT FOR YOU

Ok, now that you have your eBay account set up. You are ready to start selling but before you get started you may want to take advantage of eBay's stores. Having an eBay store means you get lower insertion fees (the price eBay charges to list a single item), there are three different store types, all of which require a monthly fee. The first is a basic store 19.95 a month, but with a yearly subscription the price drops to 15.95 a month. With this type of store the insertion fee for fixed price items is .20 and .05 insertion fee for books, DVDs, movies, music and video games. You will also receive a discounted auction style insertion fee of .25. There are two more store types that eBay offers, they are a premium store which is 59.95 a month and if sign up for the yearly subscription they drop the price to 49.95 and you get lower insertion fees. The more expensive type of eBay store is the anchor store, the fee for that is 199.95 a month and if you sign up for a yearly subscription for that store the price is lowered to 179.95 a month and again you get lower insertion fees. All the information on the different types of stores eBay offers are available on eBay. For the new person starting out, I would look into signing up for the basic store, once you have made a few sales on eBay, and understand how easy selling on eBay is you will want to take advantage of the insertion fees, and 15.95 a month is a pretty good price when you consider that 1 sell on eBay will cover the cost of the store for that month. Lower insertion fees are not the only reason you want to consider getting an eBay store. With a eBay store you can design how your store looks and with a basic store you also get 150 listings with no insertion fees, so that means each month you can list 150 items and eBay will not charge you the normal price of 45.00 dollars to list 150 items, .30 x 150, that is a huge saving, but as I mentioned before, you don't have to buy a store to start. Just something to consider as you start to grow your eBay business. I almost forgot to mention on very important item and that is, when setting up your profile, regardless if you have an eBay store or not, you want to have a name and picture that is not intimidating in anyway. What I mean by that is for example, one of my buddies has a profile name set up on eBay that is a female name, with a picture of a kitten in the profile. I myself use a male name but I have a picture of a cute little dog as my profile picture. I am not saying you have to do this but I did not notice that when I changed the picture of the dog to a picture of myself my sales dropped off a bit, I changed it back and the my sales picked up. It could have been just by chance. But who knows? Just remember that your name and profile picture play a part in weather or not someone will consider buying from you.

What is a Goodwill Outlet and where are they?

Before we get into finding a Goodwill outlet, let's cover a few things.

If you want to have long term success on eBay you are going to have to find items you can sell over and over again, they don't have to be the exact same items. You just have to have a place where you can go to over and over again, to restock your eBay store. A good way to get started selling on eBay is If you have a lot of unwanted items in your home I would suggest selling them on eBay first, it's a great way to get your feet wet in the eBay selling game. Sure you could have a garage sale and get rid of your unwanted items, but why not get the most bang for your buck, and people will buy just about anything on eBay, and if you find some of your items are not selling on eBay or if you don't think is worth the time to place them on eBay, you could always have a garage or yard sale. So get your feet wet and start selling those unwanted items on eBay.

So now that you have sold all of your unwanted items, now what? Well if you are looking to restock your eBay store we need to find some more stuff to sell. You could go online and sign up with one of those dropship companies, that will dropship your item to your customer after the customer has paid you but I have always found that those companies require you to sign up on some monthly plan, and if you want to have a good name on eBay do you really want to leave the delivery of your product to your customer in the hands of someone who really does not have an interest in your company? I personally do not. You want to have a good name on eBay and the surest way to get negative feedback is by not getting your items into the hands of your customers in a timely manner or at all.

You could sign up with Ali Baba, and find a product to resell, but I find that it takes a lot of research on what items to buy and then sell, not only that you have to first find a trusted seller in China. I have looked into it and most of the sellers in Ali Baba require you to buy in bulk, so you really have to do your research to make sure there is enough room in the selling price to still leave you a profit, remember you have to buy in bulk for an item you hopefully fully researched, then list your item on eBay for a fee, then when you sell that item, eBay is going to charge you final value fee, and then there is the cost of shipping, unless you are going to have the customer pay for shipping.

We have all heard of Goodwill stores, but most people have never heard of Goodwill outlets. When I first started selling on eBay 2 year ago a friend of mine took me to a Goodwill outlet and I was amazed at a couple of things, first, I had no idea what a Goodwill outlet was, I was amazed at all the different items they had and I was also amazed at the low cost of the items in the Goodwill outlets. So I began to research for other Goodwill outlets in the Pacific Northwest, using my handy dandy smart phone and it seems that there was one in every city, there is one in Everett, WA, Seattle, WA, Tacoma, WA, Kent, WA and Olympia, WA, I myself have only been to the Seattle and Tacoma Goodwill Outlets because between the Seattle and Tacoma Goodwill outlets I can find plenty of items to keep my eBay store stocked. Chances are there is one in your city or town.

Now let's not get Goodwill stores and Goodwill Outlets confused there are two very distinct difference between the two. First off Goodwill stores, although have low priced items such as clothing, shoes, furniture, pots and pans, dishes and sporting items, you cannot beat the price of Goodwill outlets, and the second is They constantly have new stuff coming in every hour or so.

You see the Goodwill outlets get their items from several sources, one of which is directly from the Goodwill drop off station, which are usually located on a busy corner, you will notice the 20 foot Goodwill truck and a person stationed at that that truck to take your items and hand out donation receipts. Another source that Goodwill outlets use for getting items into their outlets are the Goodwill stores themselves. When the Goodwill stores have too much stock on hand or if items are not selling or are out of season they get sent to the Goodwill outlets, and this is where the real bargains are for you and I and I am talking bargains on a daily and ongoing bases, for example in my area the Goodwill outlets sale most of their items for 1.49 a pound.

First Encounters

So you pulled out your phone and located a Goodwill outlet in your area. Now what? Well we want to make sure you have the eBay app on your phone, this will come in extremely handy when you first start out, but if you stay at it, you will get to where you don't need to use your phone, but until then, you will find that your phone will be vital for finding the value, if any, of the items you are going to purchase. As stated before, I have been to a few of these outlets and they are both set up the same way, and after talking to a few folks at the outlets, they all seem to run pretty much the same way in the Pacific North West. When you enter the building you want to locate their shopping carts or whatever your particular outlet is providing customers to place items in while shopping. I recommend taking a large reusable cloth bag so at checkout time you are not having to try and carrying everything out in your arms, most of the Goodwill outlets do not provide plastic or paper bags, some provide boxes but I don't like having to deal with a large empty cardboard box when I get home.

In the Goodwill stores everything is set up like a normal store, everything is neat and orderly, clothing is hung up, and shoes are on shelves, in a nice display and so on. Goodwill stores look and are run for the most part like every other department stores. Goodwill outlets on the other hand are not run like your normal store, in fact it's utter chaos at times. For Goodwill outlets in my area, I find that they roll out their items that they are trying to sell, in large blue bins, these bins sit on wheels, the bins themselves are between 3 and 4 feet high, 8 feet long, and about 5 feet wide, so each bin can hold a lot of stuff. When they roll them out they usually try to have between 6 and 9 rows of bins all set up in line with each other, each row having about 8 bins in it. So you can see they have quite a bit of items laid out for the public. Usually the front part of the building is where they have all the bins and where shoppers are digging through all the stuff in the bins. In the back is where the employees short through all the items before they bring them out to the general public.

Your first time going to an outlet can be an experience because you are not dealing with your normal shoppers, you see when they roll out the bins they usually make everyone wait until the last bin in that particular row is rolled into its spot, then they let everyone have at it, and it's a mad dash to see who can get to the bins first and then cloths, toys or whatever is in that bins start to fly everywhere. Some people will try to push you or your cart out of the way, but you just have to keep your course to whatever bin you are planning on attacking or stand your ground at whatever bin you are digging through. While you are at that bin someone might try and reach across you for an item that you have no interest in, and that's fine you just let them have at it, cause the time will come when you see that perfect item and you will want to grab ahold of it before anyone else does and have to reach across someone else. What happens if you and another person grab the same item at the same time? Well just do what I do and let the other person have it, if they don't let go after a few tugs. There will always be that one person who is overly aggressive and it's just not worth getting your shopping rights revoked at that Goodwill outlet. I have seen it happen on a number of occasions where two people got into a serious argument about who found what first, I have seen a couple of fights break out and the police were called and both parties are no longer allowed at that store. So remember Goodwill outlet are your source for eBay selling. You want to get along with everyone as much as possible, the people you really want to have a good relationship with, are the store employees, especially the ones bringing out the bins and running the cash registers but if you keep your cool and remember that this can be a business or a second source of income for yourself you will do just fine.

Most of the items in the Goodwill outlets are priced by the pound, in my area, both in Seattle and Tacoma the price is 1.49 a pound for all clothing and hardline items, hardline items are hard items like camping gear, toys, tools, pots, pans, seasonal decorations, like Christmas stuff, shoes, hats, and purses. Records, DVDs, video tapes and books are sold individually, each Goodwill outlet sets their own prices but for the most part they go for around 50 cents or less per item. Furniture is super cheap too, it may not be something you want to purchase for yourself but you could, and I have on several occasions talk the store down on the price of a piece of furniture and sold it on eBay for a local pick up only. So when you first walk into the store look for the large sign that has all the prices listed for the store items, and look for the price per pound, they will also lower the price per pound if your items weigh more than a certain amount, in my stores, when you reach 25lbs the price per pound drops to .99 cents. So once you start to meet and get to know other shoppers in the store you could go in with them at the checkout counter combine your items and get over the 25lbs mark and split the cost and get even bigger savings. In the next chapter we will go over what items to look over

What Items to grab

Ok, so now that you have your shopping cart, re-useable bag, cell phone, with the eBay app downloaded onto it, now what? Well hopefully you did a little research at home before embarked on you journey to the Goodwill outlet, but if not? The first thing you can do is take a look at any items you sold through eBay via your cell phone and try to find similar items, you will have to locate the bin where those similar sold items are kept or are going to be. Another good way to find items to sell on eBay is just grab an item, put it in your bin and go off in to the corner or somewhere out of the way and try and find a similar or exact item on eBay. Here is all you have to do. Type the name of the item in to eBay's search bar, after eBay brings up the items, you want to hit the refine button, and then check the sold items, this will bring up all the items similar or exactly like yours that actually sold. When you find one like yours or one close enough, take a look at the price and see if the amount it sold for is worth your time and effort to buy that item and then bring it home take pictures and then list it eBay. Sometimes it can be hit or miss. I remember when I first started out and using my cell phone to determine if an item was worthy of my effort, I came across a lot of items that just sell high enough on eBay for my business model. Your business model may end up being different than mine, I try not to sell anything under 26.00 (key word being try) I have sold items under my price range just to move it to make room for more stuff, or the buyer really wants the item and sends me a compelling enough email via eBay. Once you get up and running you will figure out what works best for you. The main point is to just find items that have sold, and sold within a price range that works for you. Another way for finding items is to get to know other Goodwill shoppers, if you go on a regular basis like 2 to 3 times a week, chances are you are going to start to get know the other folks in there doing the same thing you are, which is looking for good items at a low price so you can flip on to eBay. Now not all the regulars that show up are selling their bought items on eBay, some sell their items at flea markets or they sell their clothing items to thrift stores. So while you are shopping and start to get to know other shoppers, chat them up, you will find some are tight lipped about what they are doing with the items they find. I always found it funny to ask someone what they do with all their items and they say "I just keep it" yet they are there every day, you have to wonder how big their closet is. So some people like to keep it a secret, while others like myself, will freely tell you "I sell my stuff on eBay" But once you get to know the others, start looking at what they are buying, take notes, look it up on eBay and see if it has any value. You might even be able to trade items. I have done that on several occasions, heck once you start to go and become friends with other regulars, they will notice what items you are looking for and when they run across that item while they are shopping they will hand it to you. I have done this, and still do, whenever I find an item, like boots, I give them to an older gentlemen, and he repays me with items he knows I am looking for, I also come across Women's jeans and I hand them over to a lady there who manly deals in Woman' clothing, she in return finds and hand me stuff she knows I am looking for. So don't be afraid to talk to people, and get to know them, they can **help you find items to sell, they can be a second pair of eyes.**

Electronics. I try to stay away from electronics because to many things can go wrong, first you have to make sure everything is working before you buy it, unless you find something that is super profitable, even if it is in nonworking condition, which you can, I have sold a few items as "parts only". But for the most part I try to stay away from electronics because not only do you run the risk of selling someone an item that does not work, but it can get damaged in the mail and may end up not working when the customer receives it even though it was working when the day you shipped it, you could end up with either a return or negative feedback. Electronic items can be a bit heavy too, so it will obviously cost you more to get out the door and the shipping cost can be high as well. I am not saying you can't make money selling electronics on eBay and I am sure there is a book on the subject but they can be a bit risky. I myself stay clear of them. You may know more about electronics then I do and can create a niche in selling electronics on eBay in which case more power to you and you will not have to worry about me being any competition in that niche market.

Prices

Prices in the store vary from city to city but not by very much, the price are so low there is now reason why you can't buy low from Goodwill and sale high on eBay for huge profit margins. Here is a perfect example, one Saturday morning, when I was first getting my feet wet to the whole Goodwill outlet source game, I ran across a great find, I walked into the store with my with my reusable bag, grab my cart, it was around 10 o'clock, a hour after they opened the doors, I started walking through the bins and I notice sitting on top of one of the bine where four long aluminum tubes, I had no idea what they were, so I grabbed them, before anyone else had the chance, put them in my cart and rushed off to a corner, I opened up one of them tubes and inside was something in a cloth case, I pulled that out and opened up the end of the yellow cloth case and pulled out a bamboo fly rod, I opened up the other three and they also had bamboo fly rods, I located the name of the rods, which was written on the lower half, I entered that into my phone and found one exactly like it, turns out this fly rod was made in 1932 and worth a couple hundred dollars, I wish I could remember the exact name, but eBay only holds your sold items in their data base for a few months and this took place 2 year ago, but anyway, I looked up the remaining rods and they all had some good value to them, I stopped shopping right then and there, went to the checkout counter and paid around 20.00 to get those rods out of the store. When I got home, I did some more research on the rods using my pc and using the same methods you would on your phone, I typed in each rod individually, found the rod that was as close to mine as possible, click the sold items, and searched for my rod again and found one that was close, I did the same for the remaining rods.. So I knew I had just scored a good deal, some of those sold rods, sold for over 200.00 and if I could get at least 100.00 I would be happy. I then took all the rods out of there cases and inspected them, looking for any damage to the rods, and I found one had a broken eyelet at the tip of the rod, and some of the string the holds the eyelet to the tip was unwrapping and the bamboo tip was split. I listed all four in separate auction style listing, which only cost me .10 each to list. I made sure I described each rod as best as possible, listing any damage, I took good pictures, set the starting price at 9.99, set the duration for 7 days. All said and done I made 400.00 total, the damages rod only fetch 50.00 which is not bad when I only spent 20.00 to get the items out of the store, and the price per pound was 1.49. Once you start to find items and look them up on your phone and see what they sold for, then do a little math you will start to see that you can indeed make huge profit margins. When you find an item that is sold by weight you can go over to one of the checkout registers and use one of their scales to determine how much that particular item or items is going to cost you. So if you find a pair of heavy work boots, and they weigh 6 pound you are looking at paying around 9.00 dollars to get them out of the store, so you want to make sure those boots are worthy of your time, check the eBay sold listings on your phone, see what they sold for, if the price is worth your effort buy them.

When I price my items on eBay I usually use the sold item listing to help me find a price. If a Ralph Lauren shirt sold for 25.00 on eBay I am going to price my

Ralph Lauren shirt around the same price. If I pay 1.00 for that shirt and can turn a profit after fees and shipping, I am happy. Now remember you still have to pay eBay the listing and seller fees after you sale the item, and you also have to decide who is going to pay for the shipping, you or the buyer. If the buyer is going to pay for it you can lower your price a bit, if you are paying for the shipping then you want to price your item high enough to cover the cost. I have seen listing that have sold on eBay where the seller offered free shipping in a 7 day auction and started the price at .99, the item sold for .99 and the sell was stuck with the cost of shipping, so the buyer got an awesome deal, were as the seller ended up losing money. So pay attention when you are listing your items. If you are going to list your item in auction style listing and you are starting your price out low, like .99 to entice buyers to place a bid, remember that someone has to pay for the shipping and it's not going to be eBay.

Don't buy dirty items

When you first go to a Goodwill outlet and start digging in to the bins you will find that some of the items are not clean, infact some of the clothing items can be down right filthy, which reminds me you might want to bring a pair of gloves with you, not only because you don't know where those close have been, in when you digging through the hardline bins(bins with hard items in it) you run the chance of getting cut, I always try to remember to bring my gloves into the store or at least have a pair in my car.. But back to dirty stuff. When your going through the clothing bins or hat bins or looking at shoes, you want to stay away from items that require a lot of cleaning attention. You do want to take any clothing items home and through them in the wash before shipping your item to your eBay customer to avoid any negative feedback, you want to stay away from cloths that have stains or paint or anything that's going to cut into your time and profit. I would not buy a item that needs to be dry cleaned, that can be costly and timely. You want to take your times home wash them and list them, if possible. Some items you will not to was, like leather jackets or a brand new pair of True Religion jeans, those items are ready to be taken home and listed, after you take come good pictures and measurements but we will cover those two topics in later chapters.

Bringing your items home

Once you have your items in your car, it's time to take them home and go over them. You want to make sure you did not miss any noticable damage areas or something that will either lower your price or prevent you from selling it at all. I try to do this as much as possible while I am at the Goodwill Outlet at least a couple of times, nothing is to worse then buying an item bringing it home and finding out the armpit of a nice leather jacket is all blown out or there was a stain on the back of the shirt you did not notice, unless you know how to sew leather really well or you are really good at removing stains, you might be stuck with something you can not sell, I have had this happen to me several times. So when you get home look over the items, and if all is good, wash what you can or need to wash.

Taking Pictures For eBay

Once you have all your items cleaned and ready to be listed the first thing you are going to want to do is take pictures, now the type of store you decide to purchase will determine the number of picture you can have in your listing, I myself have just a basic store and with that store I can upload up to 12 pictures, which is another good reason to have a store, the more pictures you have the better your chances are of selling any particular item. Your customer want to see what they are buying

What camera to use? Any digital camera will do, so long as you can take pictures and then download them to your desktop or directly to eBay. I started out using a Apple iPhone that I had no use for, so I found a use for it and it became another one of my eBay tools. You can even use your phone not only to take pictures but upload them directly to your eBay account, heck you can pretty much do everything from your phone. I myself find it slower to use a phone and I like my PC.

A good thing to do, if you can, is find a place in your home that you can set up as a picture studio. You don't need a lot of room to do this, I use a wall area in one of my rooms, that measures about 5 feet by 6 feet (the area on the wall), you just need an area big enough to take some quality pictures, you want it to be well lit. If the area you have chosen does not have a good light source, you can go to ebay and buy some cheap light stands that are used for lighting an area up for taking pictures. You want to have a nice clean background, I use white, I have a table set up, with a white poster board laying on top of the table that I set my items on and the wall that the table is up against is white, so when I take my picture everything in the background is white. Now when a buyer looks at the item for sale, the focus is on the item you are trying to sell. You don't want to have a lot of stuff in your picture that will distract your buyer. If you don't have a place inside you home you could use your garage or just go outside. The guy that got me started in this business takes all his pictures outside, the light outside is natural and makes for awesome pictures, just make sure there is not to much going on in the background fo your picture that my distract your buyer. Up here in the Seattle area, it tends to rain a lot, I rather take mine in side, It really does not matter but you do want to make sure you have good lighting and few distractions in your pictures.

A couple of tools that I use to show case my items are manniquines. I have a torso manniquines and a head manniquine, I use the torso for shirts, jackets and vest, again I make sure I have a white background and the item I am trying to sell is well lit. The head manniquine is used for selling hats. Now when you take your pictures you want to take as many as ebay will allow you to, take a front picture, a back picture, take pictures of both sides, take a top view and bottom view picture. If your item is a jacket make sure you try to take a picture of the inside, people like so if there are any pockets on the inside of the jacket and they also want see the quality of the jacket. Make sure you take pictures of all the labels and size tags. These should be clear readable pictures, this will save you alot of questions from your buyers. When you take pictures of hats, again take pictures of all angles to include the top view and the inside of the hat and make sure you take pictures of the tags and size.

What to do with your pictures

Once you have all your pictures taken, you have a couple of option to make sure your item looks crisp and clear. You also want to make sure the item you are trying to sell is the center of attention in that picture. What I do is, download them onto my desktop and crop the ones that need cropping I use Windows but any program that you might have on your PC or Mac that allows you to crop and adjust pictures as need be. I find that sometimes I need to crop my pictures or adjust the lighting in the picture. I am no tech guy by any means so I do not claim to be a expert in this area, I am just sharing with you what works for me, you may have more skills then me, and hopefully you do. You just want to make sure all your pictures are focused on the item you are trying to sell. When you are creating a listing with eBay, you want to use a little logic when picking the order the pictures should be in. The order I use is front picture, side picture, back picture, other side picture, and if there is a top, then top picture, if there is a bottom, then bottom picture, then the inside pictures, then pictures of tags. You don't have to do it this way by any means. This is more or less a guide to help you get started, once your up and running you will know what works for you and what does not based on your sales, and that goes for everything.

Taking Measurements of Clothing

When you are first starting out, your probably not going to have a niche, which means any clean, quality item, that is of value is fair game, if you can make a huge profit margin off of it, then that should be going into your shopping cart. Which brings us to something that can be very time saving for you, and that is knowing how to take measurements of clothing, shoes and purses.

I take measurements before I start listing my items. For clothing, I take a blank sheet of paper, pencil and measuring tape, preferable the cloth type. I put all my clothes in a pile and go through each one at a time. This is my least favorite thing to do. I learned the hard way, but it will save you time in the long run. Because if you don't list the measurements before you start listing the item, I can guarantee you, you will be having to go back and edit your listing and placing the measurements in, after a possible buyer has sent you an email via eBay asking you for the measurements, even though you have a clear picture of the tag with the size in your list of pictures, it never fails, someone will ask you for the actual measurements, and if you don't want to lose a possible sale, you have to stop what your doing and take measurements, and after all that effort and feeling like you just went through some kind of hoop, the item ends up being the wrong size for the buyer. If you had taken measurements of the item in the beginning and put them in your listing, you would not have to answer any emails and people can clearly see the measurements of your item, trust me I know, I had to learn the hard way. So if you want to save yourself some time and unnessary answering of emails, take your measurements first, then list your item.

Ok so what are the measurement for clothing articles? For shirts and jackets I use the same method. I go in this order, but you can go in any order you like. There are five measurements I take. The first measurement I take is from arm pit to arm pit. Second, at the back of the item, from the bottom of the collar to the bottom of the shirt. Third, at the back of the item from shoulder seam to shoulder seam. Fourth, shoulder seam down the arm to the end of the shirt at the wrist and fifth and final, from the pit to the bottom of the item.. I write these down in this order on a sheet of paper and began taking measurements. It goes pretty fast once you get a system down.

For pants, I take the measurement of the waist, the measurement of the inseam and the total length of the pants. I do the same for shorts and skirts.

For shoes I use a chart that I found on the internet that converts US shoe size to Eruo shoe size for both men and women, you can find a free chart on the internet. As far hats go, I usually will not list any hats on ebay with out tags on the inside of the hat, which would contain the maker and size. For purses, you want to take the a measurement of the length, height, width and the strap drop. The strap drop is the distance between the strap and the top fo the purse when the purse is held by the strap, so that the buyer will know if the purse can be carried on their shoulder or if the strap is only long enough to be carried by hand.

If you take the time to take measurements before you start the listing process, things will go a lot faster and smoother. As mentioned earlier, I try to take all the measurements of the items I am about to list before hand, because I found that stoping in the middle of a listing to get up out of my chair to take measurements can be a chore in itself.

Your first eBay listing

So regardless if your first item is something you had around your home that you no longer want or if you went to the Goodwill outlet and bought a bunch of goodies, you still are going to have to list your first item, and if you have never listed an item on eBay this can be a little scary, but trust me, there is nothing to be afraid of, infact after your first listing the rest will be a breeze and you will be banging out listings in no time, it's just repetition. I will go over a few of the steps here but it's pretty easy once you get going, all you have to do is fill in locations that best describes your item. When you click on "Sell an item" in eBays website, eBay will ask you for a title that describes your item. When I come up with a title for an item I am listing, I use two things, first what is it and second what would someone type into eBays search bar, if they were looking for what I have? So for example if you have a Dallas Cowboys ball cap, you want gather and use as much information about your ball cap as you can and create a title that describes your Dallas Cowboys ball cap, like who made it? Is it a NewEra, or did Logo 7 make it, is it vintage or new? What color is it? So if someone typed in Vintage Dallas Cowboys NFL Logo 7 Snapback White Hat and your hat fits that description, your hat will show up and more then likely near the top of the listings.

The next thing you want to do after picking the correct title would be picking the right catagory for your Dallas Cowboys hat, I would choose a catagory that has anything to do with hats and/sports. You can have more then one catagory but eBay will charge a few cents but if it helps you make the sale then a few cents spent is well worth the cost. All the other items that eBay has you fill in are pretty self explanatory and simple to fill it, you just want to be as accurate as you can, so when a buyer buys your item they know exactly what they are getting which help you avoid receiving any returns or negative feed back.

So after you have gone down the list of items eBay wants you to fill in, you will find a section where ebay wants you to describe your item. This is where you want describe your item exactly as it is. You want to list anything and everything that may be wrong with your item, if any. You will be surprised at how much stuff you can sell even though it had a rip, or stain in it or damaged in some way. Just be honest and upfront, again you do not want to recieve any negative feedback, or have an item returned because you failed to mention something that the buyer found when they received the item, the buy will fill mislead, and will do one of two things, either return the item for a refund, or keep the item and leave you negative feed back, I myself would rather have a return rather than negative feed back any day. Because you can always refund the buyer and relist the item, but we will go into returns and dealing with negative feedback in future chapters. The main point of this chapter is that you want to listing your item in a way that best describes it accurately so that you make a sale and the buyer is happy with the purchase they made, which will result in you making a profit and getting positive feedback at the same time. Win, win!

Pricing your item

Finding the correct price for the items you bought at the Goodwill outlet is actually pretty easy to do, especially when you consider the low cost of getting those items out of the outlet. Now when you where in the store, and using your phone to look up items, checking to see it they were worth your time, you would have been paying attention to what similar items on eBay sold for and got a general idea of what you might beable to sell your item for but if your like me and you forget during the drive back home, you can always look it up again. I like to do this while I am actually listing my items. All I do is repeat what I did at the store but this time I would use my PC. So if I type in Vintage Dallas Cowboys Logo 7 Snapback hat and hit enter, and then modify my search to sold items, this gives me a good idea of how much I could recieve for my hat. Now there are a couple of things to consider. First what type of listing am I going to use? Auction vs buy it now? Buy it now, best offer. The buy it now or best offer, option is a option for you and your buyers, it allows buyers to make an offer for you item below the buy it now price. Some people like to list just auction style listing and list all there items in this type of listing, so seven days later when the auctions have ended they can collect the PayPal after the shipping cost have been paid for.. Other people like myself prefer to list items as buy it now or best offer, this can ensure that my products move. For example and using the example of the Dallas Cowboys hat again, which would only cost me around 16 cents to get out the door by the way (sold by weight), after looking up Vintage Dallas Cowboys hats I see that the average cost is 20.00, shipping not included. Now depending on if my hat in the only one of it's type in both the sold listing and the live listings, I may ask a little more, say 30.00 with free shipping, Now I need to cover the cost of the shipping while at the same time make a profit, and I love huge profit margins, So if I have my Dallas Cowboys hat listed at 30.00 and the shipping cost is going to cost me 5.35 Prirotiy shipping, I am probable not going to take anything less then 20.00 for that hat, even though it only cost me 16 cents. Why because I will wait for the right person to come along and offer me what I want, and they usually do. Now if the hat has been sitting in my inventory for a while, I will go lower just to move the product, where if I had it listed in a buy it now only listing with no option for the buyer to make me a offer, I might be waiting a lot longer to sell the hat. Auction style listing are to risky for me, and I don't like to have to relist my items over and over if they don't sale. When I set my listings up for buy it now best offer, eBay charges my .30 But I don't have to mess with it, and if I did my research and set my price right that hat will sell pretty fast. I have had some items sell for full buy it now price less then 5 minutes after I listed it and the buyer did not even try get me to take a lower amount. A combination of things took place, I took good pictures, described my item correctly, and had it listed with a reasonable buy it now, best offer, starting price with free priority shipping and a 2 week return policy.

If you do your research from start to finish on each item and take good pictures and described your item as best you can, you should have no problem selling your items.

Auctions vs Buy It Now Listings

As stated in the previous chapter picking the type of listing for your item is a business model that you will have to decide on for yourself, whatever makes the most sense for you and what you are comfortable with. When I first started out I was doing Auction style listing only, but as I learned and became more comfortable with listing items I soon switched from auction style listings to buy it now, then I discovered buy it now or best offer and I list all my items in this manner.. When I sit down to list Items I usually list no less then 10 items in one sitting. For me listing is the most boring part of selling Goodwill Items on eBay. The fun part is going to the Goodwill outlets and buying the items, taking pictures is also fun, but taking measurements and listing items are the two jobs I should probably hire out in this whole process.

Auctions vs Buy it now listings. All I can say about this chapter is that you have to decide what your business model is going to look like? Do you want to set all your items up for auction and list your items once a week and at the end of the Auctions collect your money and pay your eBay balance, or do you want to list everything as buy it now, buy it now or best offer, and list your items anytime you want and when a buyer sees your items they can buy it right then and there and not have to wait for the auction to end and also risk losing the item to another buyer. It's up too you, either way works. It just a business model decision.

Returns Vs No Returns

When you set up your listings one of the things eBay gives you an option to do is to offer your buyers the option to return items they purchased. You will find this option down towards the bottom of the listing page. A couple of things to keep in mind. eBay has set up a buyer protection program. If a customer is not happy with any item they have purchase they can return it, but they will have to open up a case against you in order to do that, If they have not sent you an email first asking you if they can return the item. eBay has set into place some great tools for you as a seller to take advantage of the return option for buyers. I myself offer returns on all my items with in the first two weeks after the buyer has purchased and recieved the item. I also have my return policy set up so that there is a 20% restocking fee for all return items but if I listed an item, and failed to notice some damaged and did not list that damage in my description then I will give that buyer a full refund. But on most returns I charge a 20% restocking fee which comes out of the refund I give the buyer once I have recieved and inspected the item the buyer returned. eBay will also place your item up higher in the rankings if you offer your buyers a return option, and you will definitely receive more sales if you have a return option, buyers will feel more comfortable buying from you, then they would buying from someone who does not offer returns. It's just good business practice to offer returns. You will sell more items and if you have a restocking fee, you actually come out ahead, because not only do you have the item back, but you make a little money from that returned and you can always relist it and sell the item again.

Free Shipping

Another great tool eBay has set up for sellers is the ability to print shipping labels directly from eBays site. All you have to do is after you have your PayPal account link up to eBay, is link your printer up to eBays shipping. Now you can use pretty much any printer to print lables off of eBay's site. Not only does eBay offer you the ability to ship directly from their site, but they also give you a shipping discount to do it. Nothing more time consuming and annoying then standing in line at the post office in order to ship an item to your customer and paying full price to do it. I myself started out using a HP all in one printer, but if you do a lot of shipping and use a regular printer that uses 8 x 11 paper then you are going to find that cutting the labels out of that 8 x 11 sheet of papaer and then having to tape it on to your shipping box can be time consuming. After a few months of doing this I purchase a Dymo printer which is a thermal printer that is super fast, small and requires no ink to print the label, it also uses self sticking labels. When I print labels using the Dymo thermal printer, it print them out in perfect size, all I have to is peel and stick the label to the box, rather then cutting and taping, it can save you a lot of time, paper, ink and tape. But when your first starting out I would suggest just using whatever printer you have on hand, because when you start making sales you will be so excited like I was, you will be happy to cut and tape labels. I switched to a thermal printer cause it saves me money, I don't have to spent money on ink, paper and I use a lot less tape. I only have to pay for the labels which I order from a website, which are delivered to my home and if I am paying attention to my stock of labels I have on hand and start getting low, I can order in advanced so I always have some on hand.

Shipping your items fast is a great way to build a good reputation with your sellers and you will find you will get positive feed back from those customers that bought from. I ship all my items out Priority shipping, I do this for a couple of reasons. When you ship Priority you are making sure your customer is getting their items fast, which leads to positive feedback, your item is also covered by insurance, so if your items is lost in the mail, and it does happen, you will be covered. Another reason I use Priority shipping is that I order all my shipping supplies from USPS free of charge and they ship them directly to my front door, agains it saves me time and money.

When listing my items I offer free priority shipping. Free because your items will be listed higher in the listings, customer are more likely to buy if you offer free shipping and if its free priority shipping you stand out from anyone else that may be selling a similar item. This is a business model I have been using for a while and it works great for me, I just add the amount it is going to cost me to ship a item into the price of that item. So if I am selling a hat for 26.00 and eBay charges me 5.35 (after a discount) to ship a hat out in a 7 x 7 x 6 priority box, I am still making a little over 20.00 dollars on that hat, not counting the final value fee eBay charges after making a sell. If I paid .16 for a hat and make 18.00 off that

hat when it's all said and done then I am happy because I still made a huge profit off of that hat. I just let my money build up in PayPal and use that money to go buy more stuff or expand my business in other areas. So when it comes to shipping items to your customers it just a matter which business model you have. The only thing that matters is that you have happy customers and your are making a profit.

What Shipping Company to Use

When it comes to which shipping companies to use it really comes down to price and convenience. I use USPS cause there is a Post Office super close to my house, and I order my supplies directly from their website, which is USPS.com. but you can use whatever method is good for you. As far as shipping directly from eBay they have a few options, you can use either USPS or ups. Which ever is the most convenient and cost effective is the one you should go with.

Dealing with Returns

Once you begin selling items and shipping items, you are going to get returns, it's just part of doing business, but what you want to do, is try to get the least amount of returns as possible. Receiving returns is always better then getting negative feedback in my opinion. With returns you alway have the option to resell the item, and with returns the customer is not allowed to leave negative feedback, the only draw back to returns is having to refund the buyer and relisting the item, once you have recieved and inspected the item. If Someone returns a item and you inspect it and you find that the item was damaged by the customer the first thing you want to do is open up a case against them and call eBay up directly and let them know what is going on. It is always important to inspect any items that has been returned to you for possible damages. If you set up your listing correctly and offered your customers a return option with a 20% return fee then returns are easy to deal with and should not be looked at as a negative thing, its just part of doing business on eBay.

Dealing with Scammers

This is not something you have to deal with much anymore on eBay, but it is
something you want to be aware of. You want to protect your business as much as
possible. Aside from the few PayPal false claims, I have not had anyone try to
scam me yet and eBay has set up a seller protection program so we as seller are
also protected, that being said, if you feel for any reason you have been scammed
by a buyer, like for example, you are selling a authentic coach purse, a buyer,
buys it but then ask for a return, when you recieve the returned coach purse, you
noticed that the purse they sent back as a return is a knock off coach purse, well
good thing you took accurate pictures of your item, now what you want to do is
open up a case and I would suggest you also call eBay up directly and let them
know what is going on, they may ask you to take picture of the knock off purse so
that they can compare the two. I found that if you provide free shipping, offer a
return policy with a 20% restocking fee, this reduces returns which also may play
a part of why I have never been scammed. I am not saying that it's not going to
happen but I have taken steps to prevent it from happening, another thing you
can set up to help protect you against scammers is to not allow anyone that has
no feedback to purchase or make a bid or make offers on your items. You can also
choose to not allow anyone to purchase your item that has fewer then say 10
feedbacks. Scammers usually work from a eBay profile they just set up so that
they can run around on eBay and try to take advantage of seller and how you spot
a possible scammer is someone who has zero feedback. I am not saying all
profiles with zero feed back are scammers, but I am not taking any chances.

Dealing with Negative Feedback

Negative feedback is something you want to avoid if at all possible and one way of doing that is making sure you have listed your item correctly and accurately. Fast shipping and a good price also play a part in what type of feedback you will recieve from a buyer. Obviously the more positive feedback you have the better your reputation will be as a seller. Having negative feedback does not mean that people will not buy from you. Not everyone holds feedback in high regard like eBay does, that being said the fewer negative feedbacks you have attached to your profile the better. Sometimes you may run a across a situation where someone left you unfair or vulgar feedback or down right lied. In that case you want to call eBay up directly and have the feedback removed. I can think of three occasions where I did exactly that. eBay's customer support is really good to work with and I have always found then to be helpful. Make sure you have there phone number on hand, like I said I have found them to very helpful or several occasions..

If you as a seller are doing your job, which is making happing customers, you will recieve your fair share of positive feedback and make money in the process.

Rinse, Repeat and Grow Your Business

Once you start selling Goodwill Items on ebay for huge profits margins there is only one thing left to do and this is repeat the process. Just keep doing it. Want to make more money? Increase the amount of items you are listing on eBay. Once you income starts to grow you may want to take that money and grow your eBay business in other areas. You may want to start selling on other sites like Etsy or try selling on Amazon. There are plenty of ways to make money on the internet. eBay is a great place to start. Once your successful on eBay, branch out use what you have learned on eBay take that info and apply it to another platform.

Conclusion

Thank you again for downloading this book! Selling Goodwill Items on eBay.

I believe that if you put this information to use, you will be a successful eBayer.

All you need to do is start with one item.

Join my FREE book club! As soon as I publish another book I will send you a link so that you can download it to your Kindle device and read for free. <u>Click here!</u>

Take a look at my other books:

<u>HOW TO HAVE A SUCCESSFUL GARAGE SALE</u>

<u>GARAGE SALES and YARD SALES</u>

Finally, if you enjoyed this book, then I'd like to ask you for a favor, would you be kind enough to leave review for this book on Amazon? It'd be greatly appreciated!

Thank you and good luck!

Sally Parker